50 Rules
to Keep a Client
Happy

50 Rules
to Keep a Client
Happy

Fred. C. Poppe

1817

HARPER & ROW, PUBLISHERS, New York
Cambridge, Philadelphia, San Francisco, Washington
London, Mexico City, São Paulo, Singapore, Sydney

FIRST EDITION

Designer: Michael Meyer

Library of Congress Cataloging-in-Publication Data

Poppe, Fred C.
    50 rules to keep a client happy.

    1. Advertising agencies.   2. Customer relations.   I. Title.   II. Title: Fifty
rules to keep a client happy.
HF6178.P66   1987   659.1′125   87-45139
ISBN 0-06-015779-8

---

88 89 90 91 92 HC 10 9 8 7 6 5 4 3 2 1

TO GRACE, LAURA, FRED, ALF and JOHN
THE FABULOUS FIVE

TABLE OF CONTENTS

FOREWORD

I know nothing about the ad agency business.

This may be why Fred Poppe, who describes himself as a onetime "incompetent mail boy" for Fuller & Smith & Ross and has gone on to somewhat better things, asked me to write the foreword to his book, assuming I would bring to it a certain innocence.

The same tortured reasoning may have brought me to *Ad Age* as a columnist about ten years ago, the paper's proprietor, Rance Crain, assuring me he had lots of people on the staff who knew everything, and that I might be a refreshing addition.

I don't recall where I first met Mr. Poppe. I am reasonably certain it was in a select watering hole in Manhattan. It is at such places I have long believed the best work is done, the most brilliant notions conceived, the profitable deals closed. Mr. Poppe's book, with its "50 rules to keep a client happy," hints of such establishments. His ideas are so keen, so pungent, so amiably *right*, that you sense many of them were first jotted down on old matchbook covers and paper cocktail napkins.

You don't get good, pointed, sensible stuff like this out of word processors.

There is about Mr. Poppe's "50 rules" a hard practicality: see your client regularly, inhabit the crawl spaces of his mind, know who the competition is, do your homework, be on time, pay your bills, be loyal, read the trade papers, learn to listen, do good work cheap.

Such things seem obvious. Listen, I have been a reporter and an editor and a publisher and a columnist and a television correspondent and a copyboy and I have worked for Macy's and gone to war, and I can tell you that in every one of those jobs it is the obvious things people neglect to do that screw everything up.

Mr. Poppe admits one of his heroes is David Ogilvy. Welcome to the club. He likes Ogilvy's writing. Mr. Poppe doesn't do badly along these lines himself. It is one thing to offer advice; quite another to do it stylishly and with grace. And yet quite another to do it briefly. The toughest writing isn't the 400-page book; it's the 600-word essay.

Hemingway said it's what you leave out that makes a story work. Emerson said we ought to write about what we know.

Fred Poppe knows. And he knows what to leave out and what to put in.

His rules of order in the ad business are specifically that, the important ways in which an agency keeps its clients and keeps them happy. But so much of what he suggests is so eminently commonsensical, I wonder whether this book of his might not have broader implications. Hollywood, for example, might well heed one of his "50 rules," the one called "Don't go over budget." Wall Street might take to heart the Poppe stricture on "sportsmanship," not cheating. And I guess all of us, even in the news business, might profit from his suggestions about friendship and note-taking and standard operating procedures.

You may not agree with every one of the "50 rules." But they are going to get you thinking. Which is what good conversation over a meal or a drink, or a good book, ought to do.

And that's what I think Fred Poppe has done here, in these bits and pieces assembled, matchbook cover-style, out of professional life lived in the right places with the right people working in the right jobs. In fact, armed with his own sage counsel, I'll bet that if Fred were back there today at Fuller & Smith & Ross in the mailroom, he'd be one hell of a mail boy. Or just about anything else they had to offer.

—James Brady

PREFACE

Because I'm an ardent David Ogilvy admirer and because I am as obsessed as David is in writing and keeping lists, I have prepared yet another list. In this one, I have had to fall back on some thirty plus years of experience picked up while working in advertising agencies like Fuller & Smith & Ross, Inc. (where I served as a rather incompetent mail boy), G.M. Basford Co., Donahue & Coe, Inc., T.N. Palmer Inc., de Garmo Inc., and Poppe Tyson Inc. (now a division of Lorimar Telepictures).

Unlike Ogilvy, whose specialty was and still is the creative end of the advertising business, my forte has been the account handling side of the business. Had I known at the start that Ogilvy's talents would eventually lead him to found a 3.3-billion-dollar-a-year international agency plus the ownership of a 14th-century medieval 37-bedroom chateau, replete with its own dungeons, I perhaps would have opted for creative rather than account management work.

However, after having lived through many thousands of disasters, dilemmas and dilettantes, I have learned the rudiments of account managementship. I can boast with pride the fact that I have handled more than one account for over twenty-five years. Also—I've been lucky enough to have been rehired to handle a number of accounts from which I had been fired.

And so it is with great pleasure that I give you my own personal, secret list of sure-fire methods of keeping account attrition to an absolute minimum.

Try them, you'll like them.

And—so will your clients.

50 Rules
to Keep a Client
Happy

PRODUCT KNOWLEDGE

Crawl all over the customer's products and/or services. Know them at least as well as your client contact does and you'll be much more adept at counseling him or her when problems and opportunities arise. This will give you a tremendous advantage over your competitors who may be trying to dislodge you from the account and gives your client the greatest excuse in the world for continuing to retain you. The customer can always tell your competitors (and the boss) that it's smart to keep you because you know their business intimately and it would require a lot of work and effort and be very costly to train and teach the business to a new supplier.

If you've been in a client relations business for a while, by now you're probably used to hearing the repetitious old client admonishment that *their business is absolutely unlike anyone else's.* If you're new to account management, don't believe a word of it! (Just pretend to.) My associates and I have handled:

- Trojans condoms (family planning and conception control)
- The Kienest quintuplets (unplanned family and no control at all)
- The Aluminum Association (lightweight aluminum products)
- American Iron and Steel Institute (long lasting, heavyweight steel products)
- Union Carbide (products for speedy microwave cooking)
- Ben Benson's Restaurant (slowly cooked, succulent steak and lobster dinners)
- Denon Corp. (calculators and automated office equipment)
- Olsten Temporary Services (human office equipment)

15

- U.S. Mint (for making your money)
- Wells Fargo (for guarding your money)
- Dollar Dry Dock (for saving your money)
- United States Lines (for shipping your products)
- Finnair (for flying your products)
- Abex (for railroading your products)
- And on, and on and on!

That's quite a diverse group of businesses but they're actually all quite similar: They all have "unique" problems that need fixing. They all have competitors who are giving them AGITA. They all have bosses or parent companies and lawyers and accountants who are impossible to work with. And—they all have too little money to spend. Yes, and they're all bottom line oriented.

So what else is new?

KEEP CLIENTS INFORMED—
ABOUT THEMSELVES
AND THEIR COMPETITORS

It's important to become a fact gathering service on what's happening in your client's industry. But, it's also smart to be a news source of what's going on inside the client's own organization. Chances are you travel to client plants, branch offices, warehouses, distributors and sales or service outlets throughout the country and abroad. Without appearing to be a "busy-body", be sure to let client headquarters know where there are problems and unrest in the field. You can be a big service in this regard because very often members of the same company will not talk as freely to each other as they would to an outsider. As an outside counselor and supplier, you owe it to your client to know some of the things that are going on "out in the trenches."

Uppermost in a client's mind is what the competition is doing. Keep alert for news of client competitors' new hirings, new price structures, new products, new R&D projects, new acquisitions, new plants or modernization activities. When you're privy to this kind of information, immediately send it, in writing, to the client and his or her boss as well. Be sure to send it in writing because if you're the original tipster you'll get the credit for it. And, it doesn't hurt to let the client management know that you keep on your toes. Awareness of competitive goings-on in the marketplace can put you one step ahead of *your* competitors!

KEEP CLIENTS INFORMED—
ABOUT YOU

Whenever something new has happened, or is going to happen to you or your company, be sure to phone or write to let the client know what's going on. If you have won a new account, added a new office, bought a new plant or hired a new heavyweight, tell your client about it. If it's really important news such as merging with another company or acquiring one, be sure to fill your client in *before* the deal occurs or as soon as you are able to divulge the information. Make sure everyone of importance in your client's organization knows what's happening at your company before they read about it or hear about it via the grapevine. There's nothing worse than letting clients feel like second hand citizens insofar as news about you and your company is concerned.

CONSTANT CONTACT

Even though you might be the world's greatest sales person, account representative, counselor, service person, supplier, broker or account executive, to the client paying your bills, it often comes down to "what have you done for me lately?" For some reason or other the out-of-sight, out-of-mind syndrome predominates the client psyche. It is therefore important that you make sure the client feels you are thinking only of him or her and their company 24 hours a day. Be sure your client gets something pertinent in the mail from you, besides your call report, at least once a week. You must let your client people feel they are constantly on your mind. Send clients something on your letterhead even if their company is located in the same city, or for that matter even if it is in the same building.

MORE CONTACT

Depending on the business you're in, phone your client daily, weekly or whatever the industry norm is. As an ad man, I make it a point to phone daily. If the client is away from his or her desk or on a trip out of town, be sure to have the secretary take down your name, company and phone number plus a message that you called. If clients are busy, obviously you don't want to waste their time with idle chit chat but, then again, you don't want to lose the account because the client claims you never paid any attention to them. Sometimes it may even be worthwhile to make up an excuse to call just to let them know you're thinking of them. Without *constant contact* and *more,* someday you might get a client phone call telling you your contact days are over insofar as this particular client is concerned.

In some rare cases, a client may be terribly difficult to reach. I had one customer who was always too busy to talk to me by telephone or to see me. She never returned my phone calls to schedule a meeting. The problem was, every three months or so she would let me or one of my assistants know that she felt we were not spending enough time servicing her account. I finally got around this problem by just dropping by. It was a big account and I didn't want to lose it so at every convenient opportunity I called on her, no matter where she was. I once flew from New York to Las Vegas to drop by and visit her at her company booth at an important industry trade show. I told her I was there just to check up on what her competitors were showing in their booths. The client not only loved the fact that I did this on my own, she implored me to stay a few extra days and help staff her booth. And—she picked up the whole tab, air travel and all.

REQUIRED READING

Read all the trade publications devoted to your business and, by all means, read everything you can get your hands on that pertains to your client's business. Read news items, "how to" stories, editorials and advertisements as well. Especially read your client's ads and the competition's. You are supposed to be a part of the client's family and as such you're expected to know what is going on at all times. If the client is remiss in filling you in on corporate details, it's up to you to absorb this kind of information from outside sources. Books, magazines, newspapers and data bases such as *Nexus* and *Lexus* are a good place to start. A well informed, intelligent supplier is an extremely important client asset.

While you're reading, make a practice of clipping the most pertinent material and putting it into an editorial file. Make and keep copies of everything that has been written about your client, its markets, products and services. Keep a current and historial dossier on all that has been written (good or bad) about the client company. Absorb, retain and place in this file stories, articles, even recorded anecdotage pertaining to the client's three "P's"—its *plant,* its *personnel* and its *products.* You never know when you'll be called upon to recite a chapter and verse about a client's history and its present place in industry. Competent knowledge of one client's background, development and progress can lead to the acquisition of many new clients. Your expertise with a single client can be turned into a good, believable case history when going after new business.

PERSONALITY

(IF YOU DON'T HAVE ONE, GET INTO ANOTHER BUSINESS)

Always be friendly, courteous and kind to the client and departmental assistants. Be especially nice and *never* condescending to secretaries and the little people way down in the management hierarchy. Don't be crotchety. Nobody likes a curmudgeon and certainly no one wants to do business or socialize with a grump or a bore. You're in the sales and service business because you like to be with and work with people. This is basically what handling accounts is all about. Be proud of your chosen profession. As Red Motley, one of the greatest salespeople of all time, said, "Nothing happens until somebody sells something." *Stay happy and so will your clients.* When you're meeting business people for the first time, try to warm them up. I've always felt that people who tell dirty jokes can be terribly boring, especially if the teller is not adept at it. However, very often a good way to break the ice and to get new acquaintances to like you is to tell a funny story, preferably a true one. And—if you can do it and make yourself the foil or the brunt of the joke, all the better. Whatever you do, though, don't poke fun at your client, especially in front of other people. If you have a good personality, all this will be academic and should come naturally.

REMEMBRANCES

Find out the client's secretary's birthday and send a birth-day card or remembrance of some kind. Make friends within all client levels—up and down the various management strata. An added tip—don't forget the client's birthday and his or her spouse's as well. Also their wedding anniversary. I keep a stock of cards on hand ready to go out at a moment's notice.

Also, send out short notes or letters of congratulations to business people you know who have just been promoted or named to another company. Of course, do the same with clients. You never know when one of these people will be in a position to hire you or your company or at least recommend you to someone who is looking to move their account elsewhere. You never know where people can pop up. Yesterday's mail clerk can become tomorrow's CEO.

PUNCTUALITY

Never, ever be late for a meeting or date with a client. This is strictly verboten! If you are sloppy in this regard, the client will sooner or later be convinced that you are sloppy in the way you are spending their money and handling his or her account. Don't overtax your already overstressed heart by running to catch trains, taxis or airplanes. It just doesn't pay off. A very good rule of thumb to follow when traveling is to leave in time to arrive at the airport one full hour before takeoff time. Try it a couple of times and believe me it will soon be one of your best habits. Clients just don't like to be kept waiting—your time is their money.

CALL REPORTS

One of the biggest reasons for losing an account is a lack of communication between you and your client. That's why it is imperative after every meeting or telephone conversation to write up a call report (some people call them contact reports, action reports or meeting minutes) outlining the things you have agreed to do for the client company. To show you are on the ball, be sure to issue a concise call report within 24 to 48 hours at the latest to everyone involved in the meeting or otherwise concerned. Very often people coming out of the same meeting or hanging up after a telephone conversation have totally different interpretations on what has transpired and therefore have no clear idea of who is to do what next. Putting important meeting details and discussions down on paper and distributing this information right after the session enables everyone involved to have a chance to get back to one another to rectify any misunderstandings that might have occurred.

A word of caution. Be sure each call report goes to the right client. You can get into big trouble if they're mixed up. By mishap, one of our newer accounts, about to launch a big new textile product directed to the high fashion trade, received a call report that should have been sent to one of our ethical pharmaceutical clients. Unfortunately the disgruntled textile customer was a woman and, even more unfortunate, the errant call report she received was all about an introduction for a new prescription product that was a cure for moniliasis and vaginal trichomoniasis. Not surprisingly, we received a bombastic phone call from her the very next day asking us if we were "trying to tell her" she ought to rush to her gynecologist. She accused us of purposely sending her the wrong report because we felt she was "offensive." And, if you think that's trouble, you should have heard the haranguing we got from the pharmaceutical customer, a renowned physician, who received the call report espousing a new line of bouffant plastic dresses and skirts.

PROGRESS REPORT

Send each client a list of every project you have in the
works on a regular basis. Always list the job, the job number or production or purchase order number and its status
in this invaluable report. Copies of these reports are a tremendous help to other members of your own internal
account and management team. Very often, a recap of all
the jobs you are working on impresses on your client the
amount of work you are accomplishing for the account. It
will also give everyone involved a fast eyeball view of
exactly where every project stands. Pinpointing those difficult jobs that have been bogged down for inordinate periods
of time can be a big aid in alerting client management to
make their own people push jobs through to completion.

NOTEBOOK

I don't care how great a memory you have, you cannot hope
to remember every single item in the myriad of details you
have to retain in day-to-day account handling. This is especially so after a substantial lapse of time. Keep a spiral-
bound notebook. Date it daily and use it for keeping notes
of meetings, phone calls, things that need taking care of
and whatever. When the notebook is full, file it and start
another. I've got files of notebooks that go back over a ten-
year period. You won't believe how helpful they can be.

It goes without saying: "The customer is always right."
A tough old client of mine once volunteered that when he
made *ten* mistakes and I made *one,* the score was: *Client-0,
Poppe-1.*

More importantly, if your notebook entry proves beyond
a doubt that a client forgot an important detail and made a
mistake, don't be a smartass and bring it to his or her
attention. You'll only lose in the long run. Use your notebook to keep you from making mistakes, not to record your
clients'.

Don't be surprised though if someday your notebook is
subpoenaed and shows up in a court of law. A long time client of ours whose company manufactured and sold a well
known brand of condoms set up a "lady friend" as a
distributor who marketed these "unmentionable" products
via direct response ad coupons.

All coupon returns were sent to her for fulfillment. To say
the least, it was a lucrative and (somewhat) satisfying relationship for both parties. Unfortunately the two lovebirds
had a rather tempestuous relationship and after one rather
acrimonious battle they split up. Soon thereafter I got a call
from their marketing maven who told me to cancel the cou-

pons forthwith. Naturally, I entered the details in my note-book, killed the coupons and went merrily on, clawing my way up the corporate ladder. Several years later a client lawyer called for the exact date and details of the coupon cancellation. I dug back into a dozen or so notebooks, found the facts and relayed them to the lawyer. It seems the cli-ent's lovely blonde paramour had hired a famous palimony expert to file a multi-million-dollar heart balm suit against my condom king. From then on I was besieged with calls, letters and endless hours of lawyers' meetings to prepare me and my notebook for testimony. Fortunately, a kindly old judge interceded and got the two lovebirds to settle out of court. So beware, keep a notebook, but by all means, be sure to keep it confidential.

RECORD KEEPING

Be sure to keep your order books, schedules, call report books, progress reports, client correspondence files, record transcripts, purchase orders, estimates, approvals, cost analyses and other important client data up to the minute. Also be sure your client does this as well. (Even if it means sending them duplicate updated records on a regular basis.) When your client phones and poses a question about where things stand, it's important to be able to

answer immediately. It pays to at least *appear* organized. Also, keep all these records within easy grasp so you don't waste the client's time while you're fumbling around looking for a key document that might hold the answer to an important question. Most important, hold on to these valuable papers for a minimum of five to seven years. It always makes you look good when you have retained files the client has already destroyed. You never know when an important legal question might come up that might mean millions of dollars to your client—and lead to a million client accolades to you. Especially to you.

DIARY

It is just as important, if not more so, as the daily notebook. Where a notebook contains jottings of important phone conversations and records of meeting discussions, your diary should list all your future dates and post all your past ones. List whom you have lunch and dinner with and where. Jot down your T&E expense items, advances, flight and train numbers, departures, arrivals, the names of the hotels and restaurants you stay and dine at. Also list the names of the plays and sports events you have taken clients to. Keep a record of key birthdays, wedding anniversaries and the like. Pre-date them at least a week ahead of time so you can be sure to send out appropriate cards, gifts and remembrances. You need this information in helping to write up expense accounts. Don't throw them away either, someday the IRS might ask you for a backup. File for future reference.

S O P BOOK

Keep an SOP book. This stands for Standard Operating Procedure—and you must keep one for each client. It comprises a compendium of SOP memos you have forwarded to your various internal departments for action; i.e. traffic, central control, purchasing, accounting, production, research, etc. This should cover practices that are standard procedures for each particular client, such as regular billing methods, a special shipping address, or a special estimating procedure. The SOP book can and usually does contain "sacred cows" that are peculiar to each specific account. An SOP book can be extremely helpful to each member of your internal account team especially when you or your "back-up" people are out of town.

CLIENT CONFIDENTIALITY

Your second loyalty is to your client, and to each client individually. Each client's marketing, advertising, manufacturing, financial, purchasing, legal, research, development, distribution, design and product planning should be kept TOP SECRET. You and all your employees must make every effort to prevent security leaks. Any information exchange between the client and your corporate personnel must be inviolable. The same goes for your own company. You no more want your employees spouting off about your own corporate plans and policies than about your client's. You have enough trouble with competitors without giving away the company store. A good idea is to have new recruits sign covenants not-to-compete and other corporate legal confidentiality pacts *before* you hire them. Smart employers add these covenants to the pile of forms—W-4 withholding allowance, bank payroll cashing and insurance enrollment cards, etc.—an employee must sign before officially reporting to work.

ENTERTAINING

It's a good idea to take customers out to lunch on a regular basis provided it helps get some work done and provided the annual billing, sales or retainer warrants it. In some cases, it might be wise to entertain the client and his or her spouse at dinner and the theatre or a sports event. Entertaining clients and prospects at your own home or for golf or tennis at a country club is de rigueur if you have known the people for a long enough period of time to feel comfortable with them. However, before inviting casual acquaintances, newer prospects or a brand new client to your home you should have a break-in or an adjustment period. You might start off by meeting for drinks, an inexpensive lunch or breakfast. You alone can be the judge in this regard. Just be sure not to come on too strong, too early in a relationship. Nobody likes a heavy.

A word of caution. Always carefully plan your entertaining ahead of time and be sure reservations are made and confirmed. It doesn't pay to be cavalier. I once had my secretary obtain four theatre tickets for my wife and me to take a client couple to see the off-Broadway show *Once Upon a Mattress*. Because the client was coming in from out-of-town we had my secretary mail them their two tickets and planned to meet inside the theatre before curtain time. While we were waiting in the theatre, we sensed that an inordinate number of our fellow theatre goers were speaking a foreign, French-sounding language. As the lights were dimming, our clients rushed in breathlessly just before the curtain went up. To our horror and the client's amusement, this happened to be the night that the entire show was to be done in Jean Anouilh's French language version. We four were the only patrons in the entire audience who couldn't understand a word of dialogue. After five or so minutes of sheer agony we left our expensive orchestra seats and headed for the nearest cheap movie. For years my raconteur-client never missed an opportunity to tell the story about the "great" evening he and his wife had flying all the way in from Boston to New York to see a 42nd Street Marx Brothers flick. Thank goodness they had a sense of humor.

CORPORATE GIFTS

A bad habit to get into. If the account person or supplier that preceded you followed this custom, it might be hard not to follow. I would suggest a small inexpensive remembrance gift at Christmas time to the client's secretary rather than one for the client. The Internal Revenue Service disallows any corporate gift in excess of $25.00. Keep this in mind when buying an assistant or a secretary a present. Also it's a good idea to make sure you retain a record for this kind of expenditure. Most of the larger, more responsible corporations adhere to a strict policy which demands that employees refrain from accepting gifts of any sort. Many of them send memos out around Christmas time admonishing vendors and suppliers to cease and desist the practice of gift giving. Every now and then you'll run into a client on the take who will dictate to you what kind of a gift you're expected to buy. You're going to have to play this one very carefully. If you get caught giving expensive gifts to a client, you, your company and the client are equally liable to criminal prosecution. The easiest way out of this very sticky wicket is to inform any hinting gift-aspirant up front, from day one, that your company policy is inviolable: You don't give corporate gifts!

OUT-OF-TOWN CLIENTS

An important rule when dealing with out-of-town accounts is that you're in no hurry to fly, drive or train home. If clients ask you about your return reservations, tell them you are on no special schedule—you'll go home only when your work is done. If necessary, volunteer to stay another day or so. The worst insult in the world (and I saw a tyro sales representative do this) is to arrive at a client's office at 9:00 a.m. and immediately ask the client to have a secretary confirm your travel arrangements for your trip home. Your main job is to service clients. You can't do this or appear to do it well by rushing away to another appointment or going home early.

SPORTSMANSHIP

Someday you're going to be asked to play poker, tennis, golf, or go bowling, sailing, hunting or even match dollars in liar's poker with people from your client's organization. Whatever you do, be sure you don't cheat. This goes both ways—don't cheat to win and don't cheat to lose. If you must participate, be sure you play with dignity and at all times, be big about it. Enjoy yourself, keep your cool, keep smiling and be happy. Above all be a good sport—even though your adversary might be a bummer!

PREVARICATION

Another no-no. Never lie to a client. If you do, you can be certain "Murphy's Law" will hang you. Also be sure to avoid dealing in hyperbole. People who service accounts have had the reputation for years of being extreme exaggerators. (Could this be where the word "hype" was

coined?) Always tell the the truth but don't stretch or embellish it because you're bound to be caught and held accountable. Embroiderers of the truth can truly wreak havoc with an entire industry. Nobody wants to be associated with a person who has a reputation likened to a tire-kicking used car dealer. Be sincere and you will always be highly regarded.

FRIENDSHIP

Clients are people like everybody else. As long as you have to deal with them on an almost daily basis, it's a good idea to nurture your business acquaintanceship into a long lasting friendship. This very often happens anyway without your realizing it, but it can be extremely rewarding, especially insofar as longevity of account tenure is concerned. From the time you get your first job until the day you retire you're going to be dealing with a wide but disparate group of clients. If you get out of college at age 21 and retire at 65 you will have put in some 44 years crawling and scratching your way up the corporate hierarchy. In order to make your business life palatable and even have some fun doing it, it makes sense to enjoy the work you are doing. Go ahead and make friends out of your business associates and clients. Try it, you'll like it.

READ PROOF

No matter what your title in the company may be, you should be a good proofreader. This goes for all forms of the written word: white papers, proposals, briefs, estimates, articles, ads, publicity releases, contracts, tax forms, memos, call reports, correspondence, whatever. Be sure everything you send to a client is letter perfect. If a memorandum you send to a client contains a typo, a misspelled word, poor grammar or punctuation, your client will think that this sloppiness might carry over into the regular work you do for them as well. Teach your assistant and secretary and everyone else on the account team to be as scrupulous about this as you are. If anyone in your shop fails to meet your rigid standards of accuracy, either fire them forthwith or send them back to school to learn to write, spell, punctuate—and communicate punctiliously.

Depending on the importance of the letter, memorandum or proposal, it's a good idea to have someone other than you or your secretary read the final draft before it's mailed out or distributed.

One good proofreading tip is to reread the text backwards. That is, read from the bottom to the top, from right to left. This helps you focus on the words and their spelling rather than on the content. Often words read in context can slip by uncorrected. But be sure you have read it frontwards first. Very often a whole line, sentence or paragraph can be left out inadvertently when the typist or typographer is retyping or resetting type.

If it happens to be a crucially important document, and if at all possible, be sure to wait 24 hours before you send it out, especially if it contains any points of contention. Wait a full day to reread your copy and *then* make up your mind.

Very often in the heat of anger, or in a fit of pique, an author's feeling of vindictiveness and angst can subvert his or her normal good writing and business judgment.

David Ogilvy wrote in *Ogilvy on Advertising,* "Never allow yourself the luxury of writing letters of complaint. After my first transatlantic voyage I wrote to my travel agency complaining that the service on the Queen Mary was slovenly and the decoration vulgar. Three months later we were on the point of getting the Cunard account when they happened to see my letter. It took them twenty years to forgive me and give us their account."

BE POLITE AND PREPOSSESSING

There is no substitute for good manners. No matter what the client's gender, when he or she enters the room, stand up. Help them off with their coats. Hold open car and restaurant doors. Let them enter first. When dining out be sure your table manners are impeccable. Dress well and dress for the occasion. Sports jackets and non-matching trousers for men are not in good taste at business meetings. This goes for extremely low-cut and/or see through blouses for female account people. When representing your company be sure to look and act your "Sunday best."

These may be simple, even simplistic rules, but they are essential to good account handling. All of us tend to take ourselves and our appearance for granted. Unfortunately, this happens far too often. If you're serious about being the best account manager in the business world, it will pay off to be more introspective about how you look and appear to others. Before you go to any meeting, or especially that all-important new business presentation, check yourself out. Pretend you are getting ready to go for your first job interview. In the morning before you leave home and at the office just before you leave, look yourself over. Shoes shined? Fingernails and hands clean? Make-up? Mouthwash? Deodorant? Are you absolutely sure your body smells fresh and clean? Your clothes pressed? You know the drill. Just make sure you pass inspection. Your own. Not the client's.

Some people have to be trained to dress properly. For some reason or other, either environmental or biological, there are some humans who have absolutely no taste in clothes. And when this is combined with sloppiness, you have a problem. I had one business crony who combined these two traits with clumsiness. No matter how much advance warning I gave him about an important meeting, he always looked like an unmade bed. I complained so often he went out and bought a purple and white hounds tooth sport jacket. Instead of being ready for a business date, he looked like he was going to the track. I finally gave up and took him to Brooks Brothers and bought him two "com-

pany suits." From then on I'd phone early in the morning
and tell his wife to prepare him sartorially for a big presentation meeting. But the first time out in his corporate suit he
walked into a meeting, tripped on the carpet and knocked
the coffee service all over his shirt and new jacket. In the
ensuing melee, a gooey blueberry muffin fell from a coffee
table onto a chair just before our hero sat down on top of it.
In just a short minute of chaos, the trousers and jacket of
suit number one were totally destroyed. At our very next
important meeting all went well. Unfortunately our friend
almost slept through his stop on the train commute home
and had to jump off the train as it was leaving the station.
As he jumped, the jacket pocket of suit number two got
caught on the car's exit handrail leaving half of our last company suit on board heading for the next station.

A week later, on the way to a new business call, this
same associate had on a raincoat that looked like the doggy's
dinner. I whisked him into Wallach's and insisted he
buy a new London Fog as a fast replacement. As the sales-
person was cutting off the price tags my buddy borrowed a
ball point pen and wrote the store out a check in full pay-
ment. Unfortunately the pen leaked ink on one of the new
raincoat sleeves and, quick as a wink, our resourceful pro-
tagonist simply used the other sleeve to blot out the stain.

We never got the business and my slovenly cohort was
now the proud owner of two useless raincoats. Sometimes
you just can't win.

If you're polite and keep a neat and tidy appearance,
you're bound to impress people. You'll certainly be way
ahead of competitors who act and look like Bowery bums. If
you want to make a big impression at an important meeting,
dress for the occasion in your newest outfit. You'll be surprised how much more confidence you exude when you
know your appearance is perfect.

DOUBLE JEOPARDY

Play it smart and keep clients apart. Try not to entertain two clients at once and you'll never be accused of favoring one over the other. As a supplier, you should attempt to give each of your customers individual attention and this can best be done by adhering to a strict policy of separation. Also, this will prevent clients learning of your shortcomings from one another. When together, you can be sure they'll air the problems they have with you and/or your company.

Another warning: Keep your clients away from your competitors. If your company is a member of a national or local advertising association, brokerage group, legal society, architectural institute, accounting federation, or sales club that holds monthly luncheon or dinner meetings, try not to invite your customers to these functions. If you do, you'll soon find that all your big competitors who are also members will cozy up to your client and start pitching for the business. Whatever you do, don't make it easy for your arch rivals to meet your customers.

YOUR WHEREABOUTS

Be sure your client knows when you will be out of the office, especially if you work on more than one account. If you're going on vacation, be sure to write your clients a week before you leave telling them where they can get in touch with you. Also, if your own company doesn't have an employee-out-of-town calendar or information center, get them to install one. Everyone in your own organization must know your traveling schedule, routing and hotel destinations as well. You're in the service business and you can't service clients if they don't know where you are. A good idea to help ingratiate yourself and your company to clients is a company home telephone number list, card or booklet. If your company doesn't provide one, make it up yourself. A wallet-size home telephone number card that lists the phone numbers of every person on the client's account team, from mail person and secretaries on up, is a great way to impress clients. By giving one to a client, you are telling them you and your people are available to service them 24 hours a day, seven days a week. That's some service.

An important caveat. Be sure not to let one client play second fiddle to the other. When you're out of town working for one client, make sure the others know that the work you are doing for them is going on smoothly, uninterrupted by your absence. As far as each client is concerned, each is *number one* with you.

WORK HOURS

Don't be a nine to fiver! Especially if your client works plant hours. If your client works from eight or eight-thirty a.m. until five or five-thirty p.m., be sure he or she can reach you at your desk during that same period of time. Again, remember you are in a service business—you can't serve if your client can't reach you. Nothing impresses a client (or the boss) more than when the office phone rings late at night or early in the morning and you pick it up with alacrity. The same goes during the lunch hour. Shepherd Mead's famous bestseller that was also the Broadway hit play *How to Succeed in Business Without Really Trying* made this point succinctly, albeit satirically. In the show Bobby Morse plays an eager mailboy who wants to impress his boss (Rudy Vallee) on how hard he is working. Morse

arrives early one morning and takes out a stack of empty
cardboard coffee cups and a bagful of cigarette butts and
scatters them all around his desk. When Vallee, who is an
early morning worker himself, arrives, he says "Good
Morning, you're in early." Morse, acting as though he's
working extremely hard, acts surprised and says, "Gee, is
it morning already?" Naturally, Vallee thinks his mailboy has
been working all night and gives him a big promotion.

Nobody likes to work or deal with lazy clockwatchers.
You don't have to go out to lunch every day just because it's
there! If a client is burning the midnight oil and working
through the day without a lunch break, you can do the
same. You can accomplish a lot of good work in the quiet of
early morning or in a deserted office late at night. This
goes for lunch hours too. You'll get more done and be more
accurate with less interruption from the telephone and
drop-in guests.

PROMPTNESS

If a client phones you and you are tied up and not available, be sure you call back forthwith. Even when you are out of town, call in for messages twice a day. If possible, return phone calls to clients via long distance. They'll love it when you do. This makes clients sure you are thinking of them— even from afar. The same goes for correspondence. Unanswered or late responses to client letters will show the client that not only you but your company is sloth-like. Try to answer client correspondence by return mail. Or, if it's an important request that requires an immediate response, send out your rejoinder by overnight delivery so that the client has your reply on his or her desk the next morning. Speed is one of the essential prerequisites for good service. Obviously you don't want to sacrifice accuracy for speed but then again you don't want to lose the client's confidence because projects are always delayed or late. Be a hustler and the people who work around you will tend to follow suit. Keep on your toes and keep running!

CREDIT—BE A "BUILD UP PERSON"

One of the main jobs of an account service person is to make the client and/or the client company look good. The more you can do to build up the client and, for that matter, build his or her job within the company, the better. Be sure the client gets the credit for all your joint good work. There's a little bit of narcissism in all of us. Maybe it's the nature of the job. Sales and service people tend to be more outgoing and entrepreneurial than their counterparts within the client organization. Freudian devotees espouse the theory that sales people are more narcissistic than others. Even if this is pure hogwash, it's extremely important to be aware of it. Always sublimate your own achievements and bestow them on the client instead. After all, the client is *paying* you to do good work. So do it and let the client get the applause—it's all part of the job. Get your self-gratification kicks out of being a king maker (and the financial and promotional rewards happy clients are sure to bring!).

PICKING UP TABS

While contact people are expected to entertain clients at their company's expense, very often the client wishes to "pop" for a lunch or a drink. By all means be magnanimous, and let them buy to their heart's content. But don't be too slow on the draw. The client might be testing you. If your client volunteers very weakly to pick up a check, give him or her a second chance. In all probability a client who attempts to pay at first, and then demurs when you have a go at it a second time, didn't want to treat you in the first place. After you've worked with a client for a long enough period of time, you'll get used to his or her parsimonious nuances. Their body language will tell you whether or not they're freeloaders. If your client "eats like a buyer," you can be sure that the doggie bag taken home goes to a pet-less house. But then who cares, it's only money. Keeping the account happy is all that's important.

HOMEWORK

Corny as it may be, the Boy Scout slogan should carry your imprimatur as well. Being prepared for meetings or phone call queries and confrontations is an essential element of account servicedom. The only way to be totally prepared is to have done your homework. Knowing and being an expert in your profession is not enough. You must also be proficient in discussing your own company's background as well as your client's. Keeping up to date is one thing, but being able to recall past dates, decisions and historical facts and figures about your industry and the client's is also terribly important. A good way to enhance your knowledge and memory is by going back to the way you learned in school. To be the font of information your client expects you to be, you must continue to do your homework. Study and read as much as you can, not only at work but whenever you have the chance, at home or on the road. Keep up with "take-home work" and you'll improve your take-home pay!

LOYALTY

The account manager lives a dual role in every business day of his or her life. He or she works for the client and at the same time for his or her own company. But first and foremost, you must be loyal to the company you work for. So, no matter how close you get to your client, no matter how friendly you've become, no matter how long you've served on the account, you must be true to your employer. *Your* company comes first. No corporate confidences should be broken. Even if you are unhappy with your job or your boss, you must not show dissension or let your client know of it. Your client should never be made aware of or apprised of political problems at home. Clients quickly lose confidence in suppliers that are waging internal internecine battles. Never, ever air dirty laundry in front of the client. You are paid by the corporation for this loyalty. You know who signed your paycheck, so be sure you follow this good business code of honor. If you're unhappy, resign. But never talk down your employer or, for that matter, your ex-employers. Someday you may wish to go back and work there again. In business it pays never to burn your bridges behind you. Believe me.

ADMIT MISTAKES—TAKE THE BLAME

If you have goofed, be sure to admit your culpability. Nobody is perfect and a client doesn't expect you to be right all the time. This doesn't go both ways though! If your client has erred and you have a call report or other documentary evidence that proves conclusively that you were right and he or she was wrong, overlook it. Nobody likes to be reminded that they have made a mistake. If you adhere to the adage that the customer is always right, you will always have a customer. But as soon as you find out that you or someone in your company has made a mistake be sure to let your client in on it. Don't try to bide time or stonewall it (sorry about that, Mr. Nixon) hoping it will go away. The best thing to do is face the music immediately. Call, write or visit the client as soon as possible and say, "Mea culpa." In this way, you can both get together and jointly figure out the best possible way to rectify the error. Whatever you do, take the full blame on your own broad shoulders. As Harry Truman said, "The buck stops here." Don't ever try to lay it on your company or any of your subordinates. Trying to duck your responsibility will only rankle the client even more.

PRESENTING YOUR PRODUCT

Your product and services can't talk! Ergo, never, ever send them, especially if they're being submitted the first time around, to a client by mail or messenger. This is the surest way to have a plan, proposal, estimate, sample, brief, drawing or recommendation shot down before it sees the light of day. Be sure you and the people on your project team and all the other people involved meet with the client *in person* to present, explain, demonstrate and sell the rationale as well as the product or service. And be sure you and your people hold a rehearsal and practice assiduously on how to make the presentation. Don't blow a good client proposal at the last minute. All too often a company will spend six months, worth of time and thousands of dollars, worth of out-of-pocket money and then lose the job because they goofed-up at the presentation. That should be the easy part.

It's important to be careful about the small details as well. One of my presentation rules really backfired on me and lost a chance to win a big new account. I make it a practice of sending out follow-up thank you letters to all the potential client people who attend our new business solicitation meetings. And to show how fast our responsiveness is I send the letters out via Federal Express so the recipient gets a missive in less than 24 hours. Unfortunately, when I sent the Purolator automotive people thank you notes via Federal Express they were less than enchanted by our using their arch rival courier.

PIRATING PERSONNEL

Always be sure not to hire people who work for a client company without securing the client's approval first. I've worked at two companies that have lost accounts because we raided the client's advertising department for secretarial help. Remember, it's just as easy to lose an account by hiring the client's secretary as by hiring the client. A good rule to follow is just don't hire client people (unless specifically requested to do so). I once had a client whose management began a retrenchment program in which every department

was directed to cut personnel. The head of one department asked me to hire his assistant who was slated to be let go during the economy purge. The client also "suggested" that I put the assistant to work on his account. Since I didn't particularly like handling this piece of business and since it happened to be our largest account I readily acquiesced. This particular bit of client "putting-a-gun-to-your-head" request really worked out beautifully. Everyone was happy. We kept the account for about fifteen years and the assistant became the president of our company. He was a real find. And—we didn't even have to pay a head hunter a finder's fee.

CONSPICUOUS CONSUMPTION

If you've got it, don't flaunt it—at least not in front of a client. Be sure you don't overspend while entertaining client people—especially if they're penurious. If the client sees you spending your company's money unwisely, he or she is bound to think you could be squandering their money. So

use your head—don't hire a limousine to take you and your client to an expensive restaurant if you know he or she is a penny pincher. If you've done your homework, you obviously know all there is to know about your client's business and personal background. The schools attended, degrees earned, birthplace, marital status, children, hobbies, former employers, achievements, social background, religion, political persuasion, restaurant and food preferences—all these are the kinds of things you have to know in order to keep clients happy in your dealings. If the client is chic and a socialite type, then it might be all right to resort to a soupçon of conspicuous consumption now and then— but only in good taste. Chances are though that the client is a regular guy or gal and will only be turned off by braggadocio, name dropping and exaggerations of your own wealth and social and business preeminence.

ACCOUNT PERSONNEL SWITCHING

The worst thing a service company can do is to continue to switch key personnel from one account to another. Very often management will use smaller client companies as a training ground for its younger contact people and then, just when they've gained experience, move them up to handle a larger or more profitable account. Constant service personnel turnover is anathema from the client's point of view. They just do not want to teach account managers their business only to lose them and have to break someone else in anew. Good management will hold onto people and make sure that account person mobility is kept to a bare minimum.

Most accounts abhor changes, especially when things are going great. Naturally, if one of your good contact people moves over to a competitor, you also run the risk of the account moving with him or her. So do everything in your power to keep from changing account assignments. Even if it means giving lots of raises and bonuses. Remember the status quo is often better than no status at all.

PAY YOUR BILLS

This may sound academic, but you would be surprised how many solid, big-name firms are slow to pay. Many customers are supersensitive about this. If one of your clients hears from one of your suppliers that you owe them money, there's going to be hell to pay! As an account representative, it behooves you to keep a check on your own exchequer. Be sure the bills you run up in the name of your client are being paid and discounted. If you purchase something for your client and don't pay for it, the client doesn't really own it. This can get very sticky. It not only makes you look like a bum, it reflects on your client's prestige in the business community as well. Lest you forget, smart clients frequently run Dun & Bradstreet financial checks on their suppliers just to keep them honest. In order to keep pace with them it's a good idea for you to run D & B's on *yourself* every so often. Then you'll know how you stand. This is also a good idea when looking for new accounts. You can be sure potential clients will get a credit check on you before they sign on the dotted line. If they don't it's very likely that whoever is competing with you for the business will wave your poor D & B under the "prospect's" nose.

KEEP AU COURANT

In order to be a more interesting, informative and entertaining person from a social as well as a business standpoint, be sure to read at least two big-city newspapers every day. Devour their business sections. You should skim every issue of *The Wall Street Journal, Business Week, Forbes* and *Fortune* and read the pertinent articles. Also read at least one of the better newsweeklies, *U.S. News, Newsweek,* or *Time*. Business is your chosen field: it's important you become a good source of information for what's going on in it. Read the leading weekly and monthly trade publications devoted to your profession. Read weeklies for news and monthlies for "How To" stuff. Because client contact work isn't all work and no play, the social side of your personality must be kept up-to-the-minute to keep you from being typed as an ill-informed dullard. Frequent the opera, theatre, sports events, movies, watch some television shows or at least read reviews of them so you can discuss them intelligently should the topic come up when you're in the company of a customer. Also get in the habit of reading some bestseller books and classics. One of the questions I ask prospective employees is,  "Tell me the titles of some of the books you've read recently." The answer tells you a lot about the applicant.

MEETINGS

Whenever you are slated to have a client meeting, be sure
you are prepared. Find out who will be at the meeting from
the client side and find out what is to be discussed. If at all
possible, prepare a written agenda if the meeting appears
to be a formal one. Learn in advance what the meeting is
expected to accomplish and what role you might be
expected to play in helping to achieve those accomplish-
ments. Be sure to do all that is needed for you to run a suc-
cessful meeting. If it is being held at your office, be sure
you have all the necessary audio visual equipment ready
and in working order for your use as well as the client's.
Call the client in advance to see if any special equipment is
needed for his or her purposes. If you have a welcome
board, be sure the client's names are posted on it. Alert
your receptionist to lay out the welcome mat and lay on the
big smile. If you are being called into a meeting at the client's office and require special equipment, phone or write a
letter to describe what your needs are. Always try to have
your client meetings where it's convenient for the client.
Be sure you go to his or her office more than he or she
comes to yours unless, of course, he or she prefers to visit
you. It's always smarter for you to be seen at the client's
office by client peers as well as bosses. Carry the agency
flag to the client's shores as often as you can.

NEW IDEAS

One of the most common excuses a client gives for firing a long-time supplier is that the relationship has gone stale. Clients say things like, "You're too used to us." "We need some fresh thinking." "We need outside help from someone who doesn't have any ingrown ideas." That's why it's smart to strike before the client perceives your honeymoon is over. Don't take clients for granted and do only the work expected of you. Be a self-starter. Come up with new product ideas, new merchandising ideas, new promotion ideas, new manufacturing ideas, new tax benefit ideas, new acquisition and merger ideas, new tax shelter ideas, new cost-cutting ideas, new legal loopholes, anything you feel will benefit the client even though it might be way out of your professional purview. Try to be an ombudsman insofar as new ideas are concerned. There is no law that says a lawyer can't come up with a good idea for an ad campaign. Or that a financial planner can't come up with a new manufacturing ploy. Or a stockbroker can't come up with a new product idea. A good supplier should continually strive to come up with new thinking in regard to client products, services and markets. Volunteer. Don't wait to be asked. But be careful not to become too much of an eager beaver by sticking your nose into sensitive areas where it just doesn't belong. Use common sense. Be creative without being "too helpful."

CLEARANCE OF IN-HOUSE PUBLICITY, SENSITIVE CORRESPONDENCE, TIE-IN ADS

Have your client initial and approve any press releases going out to the press that mention the client company or anything you are jointly working on. Never quote him or her to the press without prior approval. The same goes for correspondence you may wish to send to the client's management, sales force, distributors or client customers. Tie-in ads, case histories and joint effort advertising copy should also be submitted in advance along with suggested media schedules. Clients hate surprises. Your day-to-day contact in the client organization must be kept aware of what's going on before his or her boss does. Let your prime contact be the information conduit to client management. Help make your customers omniscient and you will be liked, maybe loved!

BE GOOD ON YOUR FEET

If you're a lousy speaker (or presenter) and become frightened in front of an audience, go back to school. Take a Dale Carnegie, Communispond or another public speaking course until you're proficient in this area. Once you get a little confidence you'll be great. One of the ways to build your confidence of course is to be totally familiar with the subject. Usually you're called on to speak, make a presentation or respond to questions (often from the press) because you are expert or have a great deal of knowledge of the subject matter. That's why it's all important to have good notes, charts, slides or other audio visual aids as cues. Communispond uses little cute sketches called ideographs that work fine. But—there's no substitute for rehearsing over and over again before you go on!

An added tip. Try to research ahead of time your audience and the room in which you are scheduled to speak. It's important to know if you're lecturing before a group of 20 or 120. For a smaller group you can use charts, an easel, magic marker and perhaps be less formal. For larger groups you'll need amplifying equipment and perhaps a lectern, carousel projector and a screen. Be alert for things to go awry. I once addressed a large group but my microphone was inadvertently plugged into the amplifier hooked into the room next door. As luck would have it, the equipment next door was plugged into my room as well. Part of my speech contained tapes of advice from a bunch of "celebrities" whose voices were recorded by a fine impersonator. The ensuing melee was hilarious. The audience next door was a raucous group from the local Rotary Club. Their audience was treated to a melange of advice from "Henry Kissinger," "Richard Nixon" and "Jimmy Stewart." My group meanwhile listened to some of this too but it was punctuated and bisected every minute or so by the strains of "God Bless America," "I Pledge Allegiance" and a complete recitation of the booster's club creed from the people in the adjacent room.

BE A GOOD LISTENER

The worst bores in business are those egomaniacs who have diarrhea of the mouth. Nobody likes to sit in at a meeting that's dominated by one person (unless it's a client). As an account manager you can learn a tremendous amount by just listening. Open your mouth if you have something important to say and, by all means, ask meaningful and germane questions, but try not to be a loudmouth. Above all, never interrupt when a client is pontificating. Let me quote Sperry Corporation's great "We understand how important it is to listen" advertising campaign: "The fact is, listening, like marriage, is a partnership; a shared responsibility between the person speaking and the person listening. And if the listener doesn't show genuine interest and sensitivity to what's being said, the speaker will stop talking. And the communication will fail."

And you will fail as an account handler.

TELEPHONE COURTESY

Never ever have your secretary place a phone call and have the client hold until you pick up the phone. We are suppliers and, as such, we are in business to sell things to our clients. As buyers, they're entitled to a certain amount of respect. Having your secretary phone instead of personally doing it yourself gives an impression that you are more important or, for that matter, busier than the client. Not so! It should be the other way around. Remember—a good telephone personality will really help you sell your company's product and services better. (Also be sure your own telephone operators keep on the ball. The first impression a phone caller gets of your company is the first person he or she speaks to. And that's your telephone operator.)

Be sure everyone in your company adheres to proper phone etiquette. Don't you or your operators interrogate phone callers and put them through KGB-like inquisitions. "Who may I say is calling?" is a much better rejoinder than "Yeah, what is it?" or "What's this in reference to?"

I think you'll get a kick out of this pick-up from Bill Marsteller's book, *Creative Management:*

ALEXANDER GRAHAM POMPOUS

This morning I called the newly appointed vice president of sales of one of the country's largest publishing firms to invite him to lunch. I dialed the call myself, as I always do.

His secretary answered, "Mr. Shirt's Office."

"This is Bill Marsteller. Is Mr. Shirt in?"

"What did you say your name was?"

"Bill Marsteller. It not only was; it still is."

"How do you spell it?"

"M-A-R-S-T-E-L-L-E-R. Is Mr. Shirt in?"

"What company are you with, Mr. Marsteller?"

"Marsteller, Incorporated. Is Mr. Shirt in?"

"Is that the advertising agency?"

"Yes. Now Miss—"

"Mr. Shirt has someone with him. May I tell him what this is about?"

"Look, Miss, just have him call me please. 752-6500."

Time passes. The phone rings. I answer "Bill Marsteller."

"Mr. Stuffed Shirt is calling Mr. Marsteller."

"This is Mr. Marsteller."

"Will you hold please for Mr. Shirt."

Time passes. I read the *Wall Street Journal* and finish *Gone With The Wind*.

Finally, "Bill? Stuffed here. What can I do for you?"

Shall I tell him? No—it's a waste of time.

"Sorry," I say. "I've forgotten why I called you. If it ever occurs to me, I'll write a letter."

Possibly to his president.

DON'T GO OVER BUDGET

Be sure to accurately estimate all costs before you spend a dime of your client's money. Get his or her approval ahead of time. If it looks as though client changes, production delays, increased labor hours, overtime, increased quantities, spoilage, transportation and shipping increases, or anything else is going to exceed budget, inform the client in writing, submit a revised estimate and be sure it gets an additional client approval before proceeding. Also, when submitting a cost proposal, always *over* rather than *under* estimate. Many firms arbitrarily add a "Jesus Factor" of 10 to 20 percent to each estimate to take care of contingencies.

If you and your firm continually exceed budgets, your clients are apt to think you're lousy business people. And too expensive. If this happens, they'll soon start price shopping. And look elsewhere.

DON'T HIRE FRIENDS, RELATIVES OR CLIENT'S FRIENDS OR RELATIVES

The easiest way to lose a good friend is to hire one. Very often the people you meet and see socially on a frequent basis under friendly and pleasant surroundings are not the same person in a more serious and sometimes stressful business atmosphere. The person who is the life-of-the-party at social functions can turn out to be quiet, dull, introverted and completely lack confidence when in the business arena. If the person you've hired can't cut the mustard with one of your clients, you're apt to let the adverse situation go along too far before you remedy it. And—you could lose the account.

When you hire a friend or relative you take the chance of also ruining the morale of other employees. Even if they're superior performers, you run the risk of having other fine employees thinking you are following a favoritism form of management policy. Often the reverse can be true. A manager may purposely decide not to give a relative or friend a merit increase or promotion primarily because it would look nepotistic to other employees. No matter which way you look at it, the patronage system can only lead to serious employee problems that will ultimately adversely affect your ability to better serve your clients.

Even worse is hiring a client's friend or relative. Obviously, if the hiree turns out to be a leavened meatball or a thief, there is no way you can fire him or her without risk of being fired yourself—by the client!

USE YOUR HEAD AND YOUR CLIENTS' PRODUCTS

Always help the hand that feeds you. If your client is a clothing store, buy and wear its clothes. If it sells toothpaste, be sure you and your family brush your teeth with that brand. It's even smart to go a step further down the distribution chain and support your customers' customers. If your client is a big steel company whose biggest customers are U.S. automobile manufacturers, don't drive into the parking lot in a Datsun. At one time U.S. Steel barred all foreign cars from its visitors' parking spaces. Clients are tremendously sensitive about their supplier's loyalty to their products and services. You can make a lot of "brownie points" by catering to this client quirk. When at all possible flaunt your use of a client's products or services in front of him or her and client management. Chew lots of client gum, smoke lots of client cigars and drink lots of client booze—all at the same time—if necessary, right under the client's nose. Just don't burn them! If your client gives you a tie or scarf that is embroidered with its corporate logo, even if it's outlandishly ugly and doesn't match your apparel, by all means wear it when visiting the client donor. Even more important: never be caught using a customer's competitors' products. I know a real bright account manager who was admonished time after time to stop smoking Marlboro cigarettes in front of the customer whose entire life had been devoted to selling True cigarettes. His company ultimately lost Lorillard's True tobacco account. Another man I know went to an important job interview with the president of Stetson hats. It was for a senior position at the firm and when the president said let's go out to lunch, the job seeker went out hatless. The company prexy gently suggested he wanted no part of an employee who didn't like to wear hats. At the very next interview, which was called to sign aboard the new employee, the hapless (or is it hatless) applicant again appeared on the scene with no hat. He was immediately fired before he was hired by the irate boss. As far as I know, he is still walking the streets of New York looking for a job—with hat in hand.

A good idea for an account manager to follow is to write an internal staff memorandum to all company employees suggesting that they purchase your client's products and/or services. Then send a copy of the memo to your client. It's amazing how well this little, albeit thoughtful merchandising idea will impress your client with your customer relations acumen.

IMBIBING—(OVER AND UNDER)

Those of us who have to extend client business discussions through luncheon or dinner hours get enough "bad raps" from jealous outsiders. Let's not give them additional cause to vent their rage with deprecating remarks about three martini lunches and the like. I've seen many a career ruined by "expense-account-aristocracy" salespeople becoming alcoholics. If you're entertaining a client or customer and he or she wants a drink, by all means join them to be sociable. It would be an affront not to and normal people don't like to drink alone. But—don't drink to excess! Always ask if the client wishes something first. If they demur, you do the same. Nothing looks worse than one person at a table boozing it up solo while guests are sipping soft drinks. It's bad for the reputation—and liver!

DO GOOD WORK—CHEAP

Last and most important of all, be sure you and your company are producing superior work at a competitive price for your client. That's really what it's all about, isn't it?

BIBLIOGRAPHY

Creative Management-William A. Marsteller-Crain Books
  Ogilvy on Advertising-David Ogilvy-Crown Publishers,
Inc.
  Sperry Corporation *We Understand How Important It Is
to Listen* ad campaign

INDEX